The Virtuous Circle

The Virtuous Circle

Why creativity and cultural education count

John Sorrell, Paul Roberts & Darren Henley

First published 2014 by
Elliott and Thompson Limited
27 John Street
London WC1N 2BX
www.eandtbooks.com

ISBN: 978-1-78396-112-2

9 8 7 6 5 4 3 2 1

A CIP catalogue record for this book is
available from the British Library.

Design by David Carroll & Co

Printed and bound in Germany by
GGP Media GmbH, Poessneck

Contents

First . . .

A Cambridge University conference recently revealed new research suggesting that, 13,000 years ago, children living in the complex of caverns at Rouffignac in the Dordogne (known as the Cave of a Hundred Mammoths for its 158 depictions of mammoths) were helped to express themselves through finger fluting – running their fingers over soft red clay to produce criss-crossing lines, zigzags and swirls that decorate the cave. Their stunning paintings form part of the extraordinary work found within the five-mile cave system.

Some of the children's finger paintings are high up on the walls or ceilings, so they must have been lifted up to make them or have been sitting on someone's shoulders.

Just picture that, 13,000 years ago in a dark cave. A small child, sitting on an adult's shoulders, reaching up to express his or her creativity.

Preface

This book is born out of three separate independent reviews into aspects of creative and cultural education carried out for two different governments across the space of more than six years.

The first, 'Nurturing Creativity in Young People: A report to Government to inform future policy', was written by Paul Roberts and published in July 2006. It was jointly commissioned by three members of the then government: Education Minister Andrew Adonis, Creative Industries and Tourism Minister James Purnell, and Culture Minister David Lammy.

Four years later, Darren Henley was commissioned to undertake two reviews by the next government's Education Secretary, Michael Gove, and Minister for Culture, Creative Industries and Communications Ed Vaizey. The first, 'Music Education in England', was published in February 2011, with the second, 'Cultural Education in England', published in February 2012.

This book draws heavily on much of the research, thinking and writing that went into all three of these independent reports. However, this book has not been commissioned with a specific brief from a government department, so its content ranges beyond the remits of the original reviews undertaken by the authors. Much has happened in the world of creative and cultural education over the past few years and this book reflects on those changes, offering a vision for the future along the way.

Sir John Sorrell has worked with successive governments on education, particularly in the area of design. This book also draws on many of the speeches he has given on the subject, as a UK Business Ambassador for the Creative Industries, as Chair of the University of the Arts, London, and as Co-Chair of the Sorrell Foundation, which he founded with Lady Frances Sorrell in 1999. It also draws on his 'provocation' for the Warwick Commission, which is about the future of cultural value.

Although reference is made to institutions and activities across the UK in this book, our experience is in England's education system. However, many of the arguments and examples that we put forward will be relevant to the education systems of Scotland, Wales and Northern Ireland, although it should be noted that each of these nations has its own distinct education system, which differs from that of England.

Introduction

We live in the age of creativity. The UK has built a reputation for creativity that is perhaps better recognised outside than inside these shores. We have become a creative nation and we need to build on that position in the future.

Education is the means to achieve that aim. We share the unequivocal view that all children can and should experience a wide-ranging, adventurous and creative education, in which cultural education is central. We don't mind admitting from the outset that we are completely partisan in this regard.

We realise that many people who read this book will already be converts to our cause. They share our view that cultural and creative activities and learning should form a vital part of the everyday lives of all young people – and that these activities are academically, physically, socially and emotionally enriching, whether they take place in school or out of school.

We hope that those who are less certain about the place of cultural and creative subjects and activities in our education system will read this book too. It is our job over the following pages to put forward a convincing argument as to why this area of a child's development must not be forgotten.

We have not set out to write a highly academic tome. Rather, we hope that this book might appeal to three groups: the parents of children and young people; the practitioners from the education and cultural sectors who work every day in teaching young people; and those responsible for setting policies that affect the way in which cultural and creative education is delivered to young people.

At the very start, it is important for us to share our definition of the areas that we include as coming under the 'cultural education' umbrella. There is no universally acknowledged definition of what exactly should and should not be included under this term. For the purposes of this book, we consider cultural education to include: archaeology, architecture and the built environment, archives, craft, dance, design, digital arts, drama and theatre, film and cinemas, galleries, heritage, libraries, literature, live performance, museums, music, poetry and the visual arts.

However, it is important to note that we do not limit the use of creativity in education only to the subjects set out in the previous paragraph. We will put forward the case that creative learning is something that should be a facet of every part of a child's overall education, no matter what the subject. Because, in terms of skills, it encompasses reading, writing, drawing, making and, fundamentally, thinking.

This is why creativity matters. It is not an entertaining optional extra. Creativity is needed as a thread to run throughout the curriculum, as important an educational objective as literacy and numeracy because it is a way to illuminate and understand every subject better. It is the start of a virtuous circle in which creativity drives performance across the curriculum, which in turn makes us an ever more creative nation.

Creativity matters. It is not an entertaining optional extra.

Throughout the book, we will use terms such as 'cultural education', 'cultural subjects' and 'cultural practitioners'. No inference should be made from our choice of descriptor at any given moment during the book. By using these umbrella terms, it is our intention to include all of the individual areas listed above. On occasion, we delve deeper into specific examples. Again, no inference should be made from our choice of examples, which are not intended to convey the relative importance of any one art form or discipline over any other. To read any such meaning into our words would be wholly incorrect.

Over the coming pages we will not only make the case for a creative education but also for ensuring that all children and young people, no matter what their background, circumstances or location, should experience the highest quality cultural education both in school and out of school, in formal and informal settings. This is currently not always the case. We will show why an excellent education in cultural subjects is in itself intrinsically valuable for children and young people.

There are many reasons for advocating the importance of cultural education, not least that it sharpens skills of creativity and connects to the growth of commercial value. This is not a new perception. As the UK was establishing itself as the world's leading industrial power, and demonstrating this through the Great Exhibition in the mid-nineteenth century, it led to the development of art schools, music conservatoires and other cultural institutions. While the perception might not be new, it needs restating because it has sometimes been brushed aside or taken for granted in more recent times.

However, creative and cultural skills remain a strength for our nation. The UK has, over many years, built up two closely related industries. Our creative industries and our cultural industries are, in many sectors, world beaters. They also reinforce and support each other. In economic terms they matter enormously to our country's future – benchmarked against the rest of the world, they give clear evidence that they can be the engine for growth.

The skills which young people learn from cultural education subjects help to ensure that the UK is a creative nation that can lead the world.

In addition to cultural education having intrinsic value for young people, there are also wider benefits for the country as a whole in ensuring that we produce a generation of culturally literate and aware young people at the end of their schooling. The skills which young people learn from cultural education subjects help to ensure that the UK is a creative nation that can lead the world in these sectors. There is a clear message from the creative and cultural industries that the education which children and young people receive in school in creative and cultural subjects has a direct bearing on feeding into the talent pool for those who take up employment in this sector. In addition to the economic arguments, cultural subjects improve the individual and social well-being of the nation.

Sustained investment in providing young people with an excellent cultural education should form a key pillar of any government's strategy for the long-term growth of our creative and cultural industries, both at a national and international level. It is unquestionable that there should be continued investment in giving the next generation of creative practitioners and thinkers the tools and training necessary for the UK to continue its position of pre-eminence.

To be clear from the outset, we do not believe that there is a need for anyone to be apologetic about children and young people learning about culture and taking part in cultural activities as a highly valuable part of their rounded education. While they are learning, many children and young people will also discover the sheer enjoyment of taking part in cultural activities, whether that is as an active participant or as an engaged consumer.

An excellent cultural education embraces the gaining of knowledge, the development of understanding and the acquisition of skills. Further, it helps to shape a young person's identity and to give them a greater understanding of how they might interact with the world around them. As they engage with cultural activities, they will experience a huge range of emotions, all of which add together over time to help them become what UNESCO calls an 'all-round complete person'.[1]

1 Delors, Jacques, 'Learning: The Treasure Within', Report to UNESCO of the International Commission on Education for the Twenty-First Century, UNESCO (1996).

Chapter 1

THE CULTURAL
EDUCATION
LANDSCAPE

There is a wide range of cultural education offered to children across the UK. It operates through the formal education system, but also relies on other partnerships with organisations and people who add enormous value to the education. Cultural education is vital to the reinforcement of the UK's position as a world-leading creative nation, with all its social and commercial benefits. But there is a need for clearer pathways for children to gain the maximum benefit from cultural education. There remains a danger that talented individuals fail to achieve their potential for reasons of ethnicity, financial deprivation and geography.

A wealth of cultural education is being offered to children and young people across the UK. The world of cultural education is driven by partnership, with government departments, non-departmental government bodies, the National Lottery, local authorities, schools, cultural organisations, voluntary organisations, the creative and cultural industries, conservation practitioners, business sponsors, charities and philanthropists all contributing. This partnership-driven ecology greatly benefits children and young people.

Overall, our provision for cultural education in the UK is rich but complex, and there is a danger that barriers are put in the way of those least able to break through. These young people are often the ones with the greatest need to overcome them. The visionary educator Graham Hills remarked that we are brilliant at putting up hurdles for children to jump over, but not so good at designing joined-up pathways that lead each child to the best destination for them. Every child should benefit from a properly designed approach to inspire and nurture creativity through cultural education. We also need to acknowledge, although it is outside the scope of this book which necessarily focuses on the institutions of education, that creative development starts at birth. Parents have a critical role to play in making sure that a child's journey towards realising his or her creative potential begins before the first day of formal schooling.

We need pathways for creative and cultural education. Whether your destination is to be a practitioner in the creative industries or to embrace creativity and culture as part of your life, you need the journey to be fully connected. The Sorrell Foundation expresses this as the Kebab Stick approach (illustrated), beginning with nursery education and continuing through to tertiary level and beyond into working life. Unless we make those connections stronger and smoother, there is a risk that the gap will widen and become a source of friction between the development of the creative industries and creative education in schools. Over the last decade or more, while our creative industries have grown, investment in creative education in schools has not matched the same pace of growth. Reinvigoration is needed. A greater focus on cultural education is central to the solution.

It should also be stated, within this context, that the UK's position as a creative nation has been hard-won over centuries and needs to be protected for the country's future. There are important economic reasons for the support of cultural education and its role in fostering creativity. As Sir Peter Bazalgette, chairman of Arts Council England and also a leading light in TV and film, expressed it:

'Arts and culture are the incubation units
of the creative industries.'

Cultural education therefore makes a vital contribution to industries valued as worth £71 billion to the UK in a global marketplace. We need to invest in this incubation unit at every level from schools through to colleges, universities and cultural organisations.

Schools remain the single most important place where children experience cultural education. This takes the form of structured curriculum lessons in subjects such as history, English literature, art and design, design technology, drama, dance, film studies and music, alongside programmes of after-school activities for children who wish to pursue a passion for a particular art form.

The best performing schools bring cultural practitioners into their buildings, alongside classroom teachers, to share their knowledge and skills with pupils and to enrich the pedagogy. These include artists, designers, historians, writers, poets, actors, musicians, curators, archivists, film-makers, dancers, librarians, architects and digital arts practitioners. Many of these in-school experiences are provided by cultural organisations, who have dedicated education departments, or by private-sector companies from within the creative and cultural industries.

Cultural organisations and venues (such as museums, galleries, concert halls, theatres, cinemas and heritage sites) offer children and young people the opportunity to visit places of specific interest, which can deepen their understanding of the world around them and provide fresh insight into their studies. In England alone, the Arts Council directly funds 670 national portfolio organisations and twenty-one partner museums. It is a requirement of their funding that they work directly with children and young people. Indeed, Arts Council England has this area as one of its five major priorities. This is a highly valuable resource – the power of which should not be underestimated.

Funders such as the Arts Councils in England, Wales and Northern Ireland and Creative Scotland, the British Film Institute (BFI), the Big Lottery Fund and the Heritage Lottery Fund are all important drivers in making cultural education available to young people. Their investment can be directed very effectively towards making a real difference on both a national and local level, although currently there is an absence of strategic oversight in how this money is being spent in its totality. However, the development of the Cultural Education Partnership Group, which sees Arts Council England, the BFI, the Heritage Lottery Fund and English Heritage working together to ensure that funding is invested in a strategic way in three trial areas, is a welcome innovation. It should be hoped that this model can now be rolled out beyond Bristol, Barking and Dagenham, and Great Yarmouth to more towns and cities across the country.

Local authorities have a vitally important role to play in ensuring the lives of young people in their area are enriched with cultural activities and this should never be underestimated. Part of the patchiness that is evident in the delivery of cultural education across the country is due to varying levels of prioritisation of culture by different local authorities. Although the demands on local authority funding are currently under pressure from many different directions, the provision of locally funded cultural education should be recognised as being extremely important to both large and small communities everywhere.

In England, many schools are now moving out of direct local authority funding to become Academies or Free Schools. It is important that children and young people continue to be able to access a high standard of cultural education in their local areas throughout this period of change. Head teachers and governors of Academies and Free Schools should be encouraged to work closely with cultural education providers in their area, including local authorities, to ensure that this continues to be the case.

The role of voluntary organisations and volunteers in providing aspects of cultural education is a vital part of the ecology. Many voluntary groups give children and young people the opportunity to perform, to create and to learn about a variety of aspects of culture. An important part of this experiential learning takes place in more informal youth settings. In sectors such as heritage and museums and galleries, much valuable learning is passed on to young people from organisations which are largely staffed by knowledgeable and dedicated volunteers, many of whom have developed great expertise in their chosen area. In schools themselves, voluntary projects, which bring adults into the school environment to help, for example with developing reading skills, provide a valuable service to young people, alongside the work of classroom teachers.

There is a belief that creativity is itself life-enhancing.

Much happens outside the school classroom too. One particular example we advocate for obvious reasons, as John Sorrell, with his wife Frances, set up the Sorrell Foundation. The Foundation champions a system of Saturday Clubs offering young people aged fourteen to sixteen the opportunity to study art and design every Saturday morning at their local college or university. The Saturday Clubs are free to the young consumers who are taught by tutors from their local universities; they also involve an extraordinary array of volunteer creative talent from the UK art and design industry who give masterclasses. The aim is to inspire Club members with a love and understanding of the arts, no matter what they do in their later lives. There is a belief that creativity is itself life-enhancing. The Clubs also provide a clear pathway for those who do decide to go on to further and higher education and to careers in the creative industries. The aim is to have 2,500 members taking part by 2018.

Charities perform an important role in this sector, with the vast majority of publicly funded cultural organisations holding charitable status. The role of philanthropists in providing funding for education projects is significant and this area is likely to benefit from any government initiatives introduced to encourage further charitable giving. There are a number of major forces for good in this area, operating as charitable trusts, such as the Clore Duffield Foundation, the Paul Hamlyn Foundation and the Esmée Fairbairn Foundation, all three of which have made a significant and sustained contribution to the country's cultural education.

In recent years, many arts and heritage organisations (such as festivals, galleries, orchestras and venues) have developed outreach and audience development projects, which involve children and young people with their work in a sustained and meaningful way. This happens both with those organisations that are publicly funded and also in many cases with those organisations that do not receive public funding but, nevertheless, choose to make this a part of their work.

The creative and cultural industries also play an important part in funding specific cultural education projects, with commercial theatre, music promoters, record companies, hardware manufacturers, digital media specialists, film production companies, film distributors and exhibitors, retailers, radio and television broadcasters, architects, conservation practices and music and book publishers all playing a significant role in delivering aspects of cultural education. This important contribution should be widely acknowledged for the value it brings. There can sometimes be a tendency for private-sector initiatives to be forgotten, with focus often shifting to publicly funded projects. However, many of the cultural education projects funded by the creative and cultural industries either directly, or indirectly via sponsorship, form a central part of the overall cultural education picture.

Cultural education is also delivered by privately owned providers in areas such as music, dance and drama. Much of this provision is of a high standard and helps children and young people to develop a passion for taking part in cultural activities. There is a relationship between children's membership of these groups and the ability of their parents to afford to pay. This particular sector of cultural education tends not to be as available to young people from more economically challenging backgrounds.

New technological developments mean that it is easier for young people themselves to make a significant contribution to the cultural lives of people of all ages. Access to the digital world makes it more straightforward for young people to engage with, to create and to critique products, events and activities being created both on their own doorsteps and around the world. This technology is developing and changing all the time and it is important that those who teach cultural education subjects have access to the latest technological advances in their subject areas, to ensure that they are constantly able to share the latest digital thinking and practice with their students.

Although digital technology is hugely empowering as a means of widening engagement with cultural activities, there remains a risk that the most disadvantaged members of society – particularly those from financially poorer backgrounds – will not be able to access the very tools that are most likely to widen their scope of opportunity.

For the most advanced young people who are studying cultural education subjects, the Department for Education and Arts Council England fund a series of initiatives, including the Music and Dance Scheme. It provides training for our most talented children at specialist music and dance schools around the country and through a network of centres for advanced training. This focuses on excellent provision and enables us to develop the next generation of musicians and dancers, providing those with exceptional talent from all backgrounds with the expert support that they require.

The scheme also funds a group of National Youth Music Organisations (Music for Youth, National Children's Orchestra, National Youth Brass Band of Great Britain, National Youth Choirs, National Youth Jazz Collective, National Youth Orchestra, South Asian Music Youth Orchestra and Youth Music Theatre UK). In addition, in 2013, a new National Youth Dance Company, based at Sadler's Wells in London, began training a group of exceptionally talented young dancers.

The Department for Education also funds Dance and Drama Awards (DaDAs), which provide funding for students who want to work in the performing arts. The courses cover professional acting, dance, music theatre and production schools and are studied at one of nineteen accredited institutions. This support is valuable and makes a significant difference to the career development of the young people concerned, all of whom show real talent in their chosen area. Since a greater level of means testing has been applied to the granting of these financial awards, they have proven themselves to be useful catalysts for widening opportunities for aspirant dancers and actors from financially disadvantaged backgrounds. They are great agents for change in the lives of young people.

The UK contains some of the most admired cultural education training schools anywhere in the world.

The UK contains some of the most admired cultural education training schools anywhere in the world, which are in receipt of exceptional funding because of the requirement for intense one-to-one tuition for students studying at these institutions. This group includes institutions as wide-ranging as: Birmingham Conservatoire, Bristol Old Vic Theatre School, Central School of Ballet, Central School of Speech and Drama, Courtauld Institute of Art, Guildhall School of Music and Drama, Leeds College of Music, London Academy of Music and Dramatic Art, London Contemporary Dance School, Liverpool Institute of Performing Arts, National Centre for Circus Arts, Northern School of Contemporary Dance, Rambert School of Ballet and Contemporary Dance, Rose Bruford College, Royal Academy of Music, Royal Academy of Dramatic Art, Royal College of Art, Royal College of Music, Royal Northern College of Music and Trinity Laban Conservatoire of Music and Dance. Other institutions which also provide high-quality intensive training to those who go on to work in the creative and cultural industries – and which arguably should be included on this list – include the University of the Arts London and the University for Creative Arts.

This sector of higher education trains creative arts leaders, artists and practitioners for the creative and cultural industries; they also act as arts leaders and trainers within the school environment. Without practitioners and teachers at the highest level, the school sector will be unable to deliver the level of training which forms a crucial element of young people's education and development. These institutions also train many of the arts practitioners who gain international recognition for the UK in this area.

It is important for the future of all art forms that the recruitment of students onto these high-level training courses for future practitioners is reflective of society as a whole. We should never take it for granted that talented individuals from backgrounds that are under-represented on these courses will automatically make it through to selection. We need constantly to be aware of the need to create interventions that help to ensure that ethnicity, financial deprivation and geography are never allowed to become barriers to young people achieving their potential at the highest level.

Projects funded by the National Foundation for Youth Music can offer young people from less advantaged backgrounds great opportunities at the very beginning of their cultural education journey. Youth Music has an important role to play in ensuring music is part of the lives of children and young people whose background might otherwise preclude them from achieving their musical potential. When the output of Youth Music programmes is focused alongside that of effective Music Education Hubs and other cultural organisations, it has the power to achieve the greatest impact in a local area.

Chapter 2

THE NEED FOR CREATIVITY

*Creativity is at the heart of the nation's
identity and crucial to future economic
development. We need to nurture and
invest in creativity to compete in the global
marketplace. The UK has a historical
advantage, as a creative nation with world-
leading creative industries, that we need to
build upon for the future. Cultural education
throughout the education system is crucial
in developing creativity. Indeed, as well as
literacy and numeracy, creativity needs to be
seen as a fundamental educational objective
that applies to every subject and helps every
aspect of learning.*

We began our introduction with the statement that we live in the age of creativity. We have also made the claim that the UK is a creative nation. The evidence comes from the UK's inventiveness over a long period, including world-changing inventions such as the telephone, the train, penicillin and the World Wide Web. The relative paucity of Nobel Prize winners from China compared to the UK has been attributed to the lack of creativity in the Chinese education system. But we should not be self-congratulatory or parochial. There is a global marketplace and the UK is not the only nation that regards its competitive edge as a creative one. For example, President Obama said this in his first State of the Union address:

'The first step in winning the future is encouraging American innovators. None of us can predict with certainty what the next big industry will be or where the new jobs will come from. Thirty years ago, we couldn't know that something called the Internet would lead to an economic revolution. What we can do – what America does better than anyone else – is spark the creativity and imagination of our people.'

The world's nations are in competition with each other, and increasing creativity, innovation and imagination are seen as the means to achieve global economic success. There is something like Maslow's Hierarchy at work in the field of economic development. Nations that aspire to a place at the top of the triangle – inventing the markets and products that will give the greatest future value – need to restructure their economies and education systems to succeed through creativity.

The UK Chancellor of the Exchequer, George Osborne, said the following in his 2011 budget speech:

'So this is our plan for growth.
We want the words
Made in Britain
Created in Britain
Designed in Britain
Invented in Britain
to drive our nation forward.'[2]

This drive is not the preserve of one UK political party but of all; it crosses political divides. There is universal agreement that the creative industries can be the drivers of economic growth. Following the agricultural age, the industrial age and the technological age, we have now reached the age of creativity with every nation aware of the need to harness the creativity of its people. Creativity sets the human race apart, enabling us to solve problems and make a better world.

---

2 https://www.gov.uk/government/news/2011-budget-britain-open-for-business

In this respect, the UK has an inbuilt advantage as a nation. We started down this path earlier than anyone else. Now we should not waste that advantage, and we should be aware that others are pursuing the same thought and trying to close the gap. Many of those competitors have huge resources on their side.

Creativity sets the human race apart, enabling us to solve problems and make a better world.

In 2003, the London Design Festival launched itself to the world. It has run every year since, for nine days every September, when visitors from around the UK and the world come to London to experience the latest innovations in design and debate the current state of the art with international practitioners. Festival events are attended by nearly half a million people, over 10 per cent of them from abroad. Visitors come to look, take part, admire, learn and, perhaps, imitate. If imitation is the sincerest form of flattery, we should be flattered that, since the original

London Design Festival, more than a hundred cities have started their own versions of a design festival.

Three years ago the Mayor of Beijing, Guo Jinlong, put on a lavish opening ceremony for the Beijing Design Week. He introduced it with these words: 'The ultimate goal is to transform Made in China into Designed in China.'

Creativity is integral to everything we do. It inspires innovation, improving our environment, our products, our businesses and the quality of our lives.

The reasons are apparent. In today's global economy, where capital and labour are so mobile, where goods and services can be produced almost anywhere, it is the power of ideas and innovation, of creativity and design adding value, that will bring economic success and prosperity. Creativity is integral to everything we do. It inspires innovation, improving our environment, our products, our businesses and the quality of our lives. It improves our education too, and it needs to do so more.

The world's creative industries make up around 7 per cent (and rising) of global GDP. They are rightly recognised as essential to economic success as well as to the vitality of society. They provide not just money and jobs but also an inventive and intellectual edge to the culture and identity of nations and cities. Creativity is a defining feature of the UK's identity.

So how should we inspire even greater creativity in the future?

Clearly education has the leading role to play. We believe that cultural education needs to be in the vanguard of developing creativity. But we go further by saying that creativity needs to be seen as a prime objective for every child engaged in the UK education system.

The problem is that cultural education is still seen by some as a second-class activity compared to the academic subjects that form the core of the school curriculum. Literacy and numeracy are rightly regarded as vital, almost a right for every educated child. All parents want their children to be literate and numerate because they know that without these skills it will be hard to succeed in life.

In the future we believe it will be hard to succeed in life without creativity. We believe the three pillars of the twenty-first-century education system should be creativity, literacy and numeracy. Just as literacy and numeracy are fundamental to developing creative skills, so is creativity essential to developing higher levels of literacy and numeracy. It's a virtuous circle.

The three pillars of the twenty-first-century education system should be creativity, literacy and numeracy.

Chapter 3

THE CASE FOR CULTURAL EDUCATION

Every child should receive the best cultural education. This education should provide knowledge about culture's past, develop understanding and critical faculties, and enhance skills through practice in significant art forms. Other emotional and relationship benefits result from these, teaching lessons that apply to other areas of life. But high-quality interactions are essential, with schools best placed to ensure quality and champion diversity. Cultural education should encourage individual and collaborative abilities, grounded in the knowledge of the past (with visits to cultural places vital) but committed to the exploration of the present and the future (with digital technology playing an enabling role). Although all cultural education should be of the highest academic and vocational standards, it should also be fun.

There are myriad different reasons why every child should receive the best possible cultural education, in particular its role in stimulating creativity. We have already mentioned some of the key factors in the introduction to this book; others we will expand upon later. Here are just three of the benefits that we see resulting from cultural education:

- The direct educational benefits to children through the acquisition of knowledge, skills and experiences from cultural education subjects.

- The additional benefits to the creative and cultural industries and the wider economy of providing children with an excellent cultural education that fosters creativity. This in turn creates the workforce of the future, helping to drive forward the UK's growth agenda.

- The wider benefits to our society as a whole of developing an understanding of our common cultural heritage.

At its best, a sound cultural education should allow children to gain **knowledge** through the learning of facts; **understanding** of the world around them through the development of their critical faculties and experiences; and **skills** through the opportunity to practise specific art forms. Their experiences of cultural activities are also likely to develop their **emotions** and their **relationships**. Taking part in a cultural activity or witnessing a performance can be exciting, frightening, moving, uplifting, challenging and enjoyable – all of which teach lessons that are applicable to many other areas of a young person's life. Involvement with cultural activities, whether as an active participant (creating a piece of art or craft, reading a book, making a short film) or actively experiencing an event or place (visiting a heritage site, gallery or museum, seeing how a building works, watching a music, dance or film performance) can be habit forming for the rest of a young person's life.

However, it should be stressed that the quality of the interaction is of utmost importance. A poor experience during childhood could risk putting a child off future similar cultural activities into adulthood. So, it remains vitally important that all interactions that children and young people have in this area are of high quality, particularly if they are experiencing a specific area of culture for the first time. It is equally important that there is a common understanding of exactly what excellence in the delivery of cultural education means; a subject to which we will return later. It should also be noted that, for much the same reason, it is essential that the experiences to which children are introduced are appropriate for their age. At the right time in a child's development, a particular cultural activity could excite and invigorate them. If it happens too early or too late in their

Taking part in a cultural activity or witnessing a performance can be exciting, frightening, moving, uplifting, challenging and enjoyable.

learning development, there is a risk that it could leave them either bewildered or bored.

Although we celebrate and welcome every aspect of cultural education in this book, no matter where it is delivered, school will inevitably form the most significant part of a child's education. This is particularly the case with children who come from the most deprived backgrounds. In these instances, many of their parents and carers may themselves not have been lucky enough to benefit from a wide-ranging cultural education. There is therefore a gap in understanding and experience among the influential adults in these children's lives. More needs to continue to be done to ensure that the value of cultural activities and experiences for everyone, no matter what their background, is widely understood. There are also challenges in accessing cultural education facing looked-after children, children with special educational needs and disabilities, and children outside mainstream education and training.

Cultural education touches the lives of children and young people across the entire gamut of age ranges and should aim to be inclusive, rather than exclusive. The introduction of cultural education to children before they go to school is of clear benefit. This can be through engagement with books, language and rhymes; singing, dancing and rhythms; or painting, drawing and making things. And cultural education should not exist in a vacuum; the organisations delivering it should be prepared to take cultural education into settings where children and young people already spend their time. This might include youth clubs, nursery groups or sporting venues. Cultural activities should form a central part of any strategy developed for the delivery of educational and recreational activities for the well-being of young people. Children should be able to connect to the cultural education that they receive irrespective of race, gender or disability. It is important that no minority groups are forgotten as cultural education provision develops.

When taught well, cultural education includes four particular elements. The first is knowledge-based and teaches children about the best of what has been created (for example great literature, art, architecture, film, music and drama). It introduces young people to a broader range of cultural thought and creativity than they would be likely to encounter in their lives outside school.

The second part of cultural education centres on the development of analytical and critical skills, which additionally have a direct relevance across other subjects, as we discuss later. This is especially important in heritage and history, where the subject could otherwise be reduced to the accumulation of facts, rather than also including the acquisition of an understanding of historical context.

The third element of cultural education is skills-based and enables children to participate in and to create new culture for themselves (for example designing a product, drawing, composing music, choreographing a production, performing rap poetry or making a short film). When delivered well, cultural education should not just be about visiting museums, galleries or heritage sites, or about seeing performances, although all of these remain important parts of the whole package of cultural education. Often, cultural education activities will be collaborative and will help children to learn how to work together as a team. However, it is essential that children and young people are encouraged to undertake regular solo activities, such as reading books, writing stories, drawing pictures, learning crafts and making music. Over time, they will get better at doing each of these things, as they build up skills and knowledge through repetitive practice. Becoming proficient in these solo activities can have a profound effect on a child's development.

The fourth element of a good cultural education centres on the development of an individual's personal creativity – a topic that is a central thread of this book.

One of the less tangible, but nonetheless important, benefits of a rounded cultural education is that it gives us an understanding of where we find ourselves at any given moment on a continuum of cultural development. Schools perform a valuable role in encouraging children to explore and to discover. Without cultural education in schools, there is a risk that children would face disconnection from great writers, artists and musicians. The best of these established works of art are as relevant and brilliant today as they were when they were first created.

By reading and learning about the works of the great authors, poets and playwrights of the past, we can understand the development of literature and drama in the twentieth and twenty-first centuries and the place of brand-new works as part of the continuous reinvention of these genres. The same is true for other art forms, such as music or the visual arts. The great composers or painters of hundreds of years ago inform our understanding of the musicians and artists who are producing groundbreaking work today. Similarly, the British influence on film is immense and informs much of the thinking on the way that the cinema of today is being made around the world. Whether it be names from the past such as Charlie Chaplin and Alfred Hitchcock, or the latest box-office successes such as Danny Boyle, Tom Hooper and Steve McQueen, Britain continues to lead the way in many areas of film-making. Britain also has exceptional talent in technical fields such as audio-visual effects and computer graphics. We need to ensure that there continues to be a flow of home-grown talent through our education system into this area, as it increases importance within Britain's creative and cultural industries.

Any rounded cultural education should have space to include newer art forms, which have yet to pass the test of time, alongside the very best creativity from times gone by. Children should be exposed to new practices and new ways of creating, whether this is through the use of innovative digital technology, or a new take on more established practice. The young people studying these subjects should be equipped with the knowledge and understanding to enable them to make informed value judgements about their own personal preferences, based on their learning. Schools' curricula in these areas should give weight both to the new and the old, better to enable a greater understanding of the way in which culture has developed over time.

Developments in digital technology continue to revolutionise the way in which cultural education subjects are taught in the formal school environment. Alongside this, the changing digital landscape affords young people significant opportunities to enjoy creative arts in new and exciting ways that speak to their own youth culture in more informal settings. More informal learning by young people should also be valued, as it often has a particular relevance to skills that may enhance their future employability across a wide range of different sectors, not just those in the creative and cultural industries.

The vast majority of cinema screens in the UK are now digital. This has opened up huge possibilities for the dissemination of cultural education across the country, with a distribution network that is both high quality and economically efficient. Government, schools and funding bodies need to ensure that they keep up with innovations in this area, with policy being developed that is mindful of a forward-looking, rather than backward-facing, agenda. The BFI's programme of learning for five- to nineteen-year-olds – and in particular the BFI Film Academy – is a welcome new development in delivering education activities that encourage young people across the UK to watch, make and understand film. The programme makes great use of the latest digital technology in all aspects of its work.

Aside from visits to historic sites, a significant part of the heritage area of cultural education is the creation of an understanding of a sense of place for children and young people. The implications of disconnection from a young person's built environment can have significant consequences, with potentially greater levels of vandalism and anti-social behaviour.

Cultural education in general – and specifically taking part in cultural activities – can also be a major contributor to helping a young person to develop a sense of their own identity and a shared understanding and appreciation of the environment within which they live and their own personal role within that environment. This operates on a number of levels, whether it is in a school, a community, a village, town or city, or in gaining an appreciation of how British culture is viewed internationally. English Heritage's 'Heritage Schools' programme, which sees eight regional clusters of twelve schools working together to provide specific learning based on local heritage, is an exciting step forward in formalising the importance of heritage-related activities and venues in the classroom context.

It may seem very obvious to those people whose lives have already been enriched by an excellent cultural education, but it is worth underlining the point we made back in the Introduction that the journey of discovery through culture, together with the opportunity to experience cultural activities, is enjoyable. Cultural education is enriching both in academic and skills-based terms. But it is also fun. And we should never be ashamed of that.

Chapter 4

CREATIVE LEARNING AS A CORE TEACHING AIM

Our ambition is for a challenging and inspiring creative education. Young people need to be considered more fully as the consumers of such an education. The benefits that accrue to them as individuals have a beneficial impact on society as a whole. Cultural education has a particular contribution to make in creating generations that are more inquisitive, persistent, imaginative, disciplined and collaborative – essential qualities for the future. The result will be generations of job-creators, not just job-seekers, vital for a world of continuous and rapid change. Creative learning therefore needs to be seen as a core teaching aim in all subjects.

If they are not fully engaged with their education, they will not be best able to make full use of it.

Earlier, we outlined our ambition for all children to receive a wide-ranging, adventurous and **creative** cultural education. And we have also made clear our belief that **creative learning** is something that should be a facet of every part of a child's education, no matter what the subject.

We also believe that we need to think of children and young people as the consumers of education. Unlike adult consumers they are rarely asked what they think. They should be – if they are not fully engaged with their education, they will not be best able to make full use of it, develop their potential and contribute to the richness of society. A programme of listening to young people, finding out their views of their own education, would be valuable for everyone involved. This is particularly so in the context of the components we set out below for what makes learning creative.

We have already described the scope of cultural education in our Introduction – covering a wide range of individual but related subjects from archaeology to the visual arts. It involves learning about the canon of the cultural form as well as developing as both a critical spectator and as an active participant. It involves the opportunity to develop talent and, for some, to open up a career pathway. For all it will engage with personal identity and development.

So what do we mean by creative learning? Our intuitive notion of being creative probably involves using our imagination, making something original (original to ourselves even if not to others). But to recognise and develop what makes learning creative, we need to identify its components. There are five that we suggest:

1 First, creative learning involves young people becoming **inquisitive**. Young people need to be presented with challenges that make them wonder and question, giving them the will to explore and investigate.

2 But that inquisitive enthusiasm is not in itself enough to make learning creative. At the heart of being creative is being **persistent**. So, young people need to be presented with challenges that require them to manage some uncertainty, to stick with those challenges even through difficulty. It also involves developing the confidence of young people to be different and to suggest original possibilities.

3 The third characteristic of creative learning is that it involves unlocking young people's ability to be **imaginative**. This requires the time and context for young people to play with various possibilities, to spot new connections and to use their intuition.

4 There is a misguided criticism of creative learning that it is somehow free and easy, with less rigour than other forms of learning. Nothing could be further from the truth. There is a **discipline** in creative learning based on the need to craft, to improve first attempts, to reflect critically and to develop techniques.

5 And a final essential characteristic of creative learning is that it is **collaborative**. It involves co-operating with others, giving and receiving constructive feedback and sharing the process and outcome of the exercise.

We believe that learning that has these characteristics fully involves young people. That involvement means that both the skills and the knowledge become embedded and retained. It develops the confidence and flexibility in young people to face, and flourish in, the context of continuous and rapid change that will characterise the world they will occupy and shape.

These characteristics are resonant with UNESCO's key characteristics of quality in education[3]:

---

3 'Education for All – The Quality Imperative', EFA Global Monitoring Report, UNESCO (2005).

Learning to know acknowledges that learners build their own knowledge daily, combining indigenous and 'external' elements.

Learning to do focuses on the practical application of what is learned.

Learning to live together addresses the critical skills for a life free from discrimination, where all have equal opportunity to develop themselves, their families and their communities.

Learning to be emphasises the skills needed for individuals to develop their full potential.

And we are not alone in holding this view of creative learning.

Michael Barber in 'Oceans of Innovation'[4] presents a blunt challenge:

'. . . even the best education systems in the world . . . need to radically rethink what they offer every student. There are powerful reasons to believe that what worked spectacularly between 1960 and 2010 will

---

4 Barber, M., Donelly, K. and Rozvi, S., 'Oceans of Innovation: The Atlantic, the Pacific, global leadership and the future of education', Institute for Public Policy Research (2012).

not work between 2010 and 2060 . . . It will depend on individuals who are open to ideas and arguments and who are part of teams in which vigorous debate, dissent and discomfort exist. It will require a culture of openness – to argument and to ideas, experts and outsiders, the young and the new.'

Most strikingly, Barber reports on research by Professor Yong Zhao[5] in which countries' PISA (The Programme for International Student Assessment) mathematics scores are graphed against perceived entrepreneurial capacity – the outcome being a negative correlation. In other words, while competencies in mathematics are undoubtedly necessary as a key part of a full and rounded education, they are alone not sufficient for the challenges our young people face. This points to the need for a theory and practice on 'building a creative generation' – a generation which possesses those vitally important skills of being inquisitive, persistent, imaginative, disciplined and collaborative.

Paul Collard, the Chief Executive of Creativity, Culture and Education (CCE), a UK-based charity that works internationally to unlock the creativity of young people in and out of formal education, writes[6]:

5 www.zhaolearning.com/2012/06/06/test-score-vs-entreneurshippisa-times-and-confidence
6 Collard, P., 'Creative thinking – the role of creativity in our education system', *New Statesman* (2012).

'A creative education is designed to generate curious, ambitious, reflective, autonomous adults, intrinsically motivated, self-managing and capable not only of imagining a better future but of delivering it. In the world into which young people today will emerge this is vital. The world no longer awaits job-seekers. It demands job creators, young people capable of inventing their own futures, changing the nature of their employment several times in their lives and forever developing new skills. Without this flexibility of mind, adaptability to new circumstances and passion for continuing to learn, their future is bleak. A creative education ensures activities in which pupils are involved to develop their competence (so they feel effective), their autonomy (so they understand themselves to be the source of their own behaviour) and their relatedness (through which they feel connected to other individuals and their community).'

Hoffman and Casnocha echo this in *The Start up of You*[7]:

'What's required now is an entrepreneurial mindset. Whether you work for a ten-person company, a giant multinational corporation, a not-for-profit, a

---

7 Hoffman, R. and Casnocha, B., *The Start up of You*, Random House Business (2012).

government agency, or any type of organisation in between – if you want to seize the new opportunities and meet the challenges of today's fractured landscapes, you need to think and act like you're running a start-up: your career. The conditions in which entrepreneurs start and grow companies are the conditions in which we all now live . . . You never know what's going to happen next. Information is limited. Resources are tight. Competition is fierce. The world is changing . . . This means you need to be adapting all the time. And if you fail to adapt, no one – not your employer, not the government – is going to catch you when you fall.'

And most recently the McKinsey report 'Education to Employment'[8] gives further credence to this argument. It states that the most significant differences between the skills that employers value and those they can find lie in the soft skills of creativity, communication, collaboration, motivation (work ethic) and problem solving.

So, we believe that the case for developing creative confidence in our young people is compelling. And we believe that those characteristics of creative learning should be at the heart of learning across the curriculum.

8 Mourshed, M., Patel, J. and Suder, K., 'Education to Employment: Getting Europe's Youth into Work', McKinsey & Company (2014).

Creative learning should be a core teaching aim in all subjects. There is a developing evidence base and taxonomy for creative teaching. The aim is realisable.

So what of the relationship between creative learning and cultural education? It is a mistake to conceive of 'cultural education and creative learning' as one unified concept. Some cultural education can be far from creative. Some creative learning has little to do with culture or the arts. But we do believe that excellent cultural education is a particularly powerful vehicle for creative learning. Cultural education is not unique in this respect, but it does offer especially rich opportunities for creative teaching and learning. Fully understanding a novel and building on it to write one's own fiction, learning to play a musical instrument, choreographing and performing dance – all these require a young person to be inquisitive, persistent, imaginative, disciplined and collaborative. Young people can become more creative by learning distinct skills, by learning about the techniques, views and influences of the great writers, artists, film-makers and musicians.

Creative learning is not a soft option. It does not eschew knowledge content. We should counter the false dichotomy expressed by some between creative and academic learning. The two should never be seen as mutually exclusive. Creativity is not an alternative to academic learning. Nor should the opportunity for creativity be limited for more academically able students because they are steered away from the chance to study those cultural education subjects which offer such a rich opportunity for creative development of young people.

Creative learning is not a soft option. It does not eschew knowledge content.

We should be ambitious for a creative pedagogy in creative institutions within a creative education system. This approach needs to be clearly focused on its benefits for the consumers – children and young people – to achieve the greatest value for all of our society.

Chapter 5

THE IMPACT
OF RAISED
EXPECTATIONS

Setting expectations high is important in enabling children to achieve their potential through education. Evidence shows that teacher and parental expectation is a cornerstone of pupil success. Creative and cultural education are important in raising such expectations, acting as catalysts for life-changing experiences that have a positive impact on the ambition and confidence of young people. Parents also find it easier and more productive to support their children in creative programmes at home, making education a more natural aspect of a rounded life. Cultural institutions have vital roles to play in adding breadth and depth to the school experience, broadening horizons for pupils particularly at times when low self-esteem, for example in the early teenage years, can lead to decisions that limit educational achievement.

In our previous chapter we outlined the distinction, and the relationship, between cultural and creative education. We argued that creative learning is an essential for young people and that cultural education is a particularly powerful, if not unique, vehicle for that. In this chapter we argue that creative and cultural education have an important, but sometimes under-recognised, impact on raising educational expectations – of pupils, parents and teachers. And from raised expectations other benefits follow, including a strengthened sense of identity, increased self-esteem and heightened sense of well-being.

We would go further and argue that cultural education in school creates a culture of learning. Cultural education and experience creates a tenor, an ethos, a set of shared values. Many head teachers have used cultural education and experience as an effective means of making a dramatic school improvement.

So what is the significance of the expectations that we have of our young people and that they have of themselves? There is research evidence and literature on the value of setting high expectations and the common unconscious slip by teachers into underestimating pupil potential. The study by Rutter, *Fifteen Thousand Hours*[9], reported on a number of London schools

---

9 Rutter, M., *Fifteen Thousand Hours: Secondary Schools and Their Effects on Children*, Harvard University Press (1982).

in deprived areas and suggested the recalibration of teacher expectation was a key to fostering well-being and achievement among disadvantaged children. There are many behavioural studies from North America and Canada showing that teacher expectation has a dramatic effect on achievement.[10]

As the dates of these reports indicate, we have known for a long time that expectation is a cornerstone of pupil success.

Our contention in this chapter is that creative and cultural education is one of the most effective catalysts for the vital life-chemistry of ambition, confidence and expectation. Creative and cultural education unlocks expectation. It unlocks heightened expectation for young people of themselves. Even more powerfully, it unlocks the expectations placed by teachers, parents and carers in young people. And those heightened expectations are self-fulfilling. Never has this been a more important virtuous circle to create and sustain given the challenges and uncertainties that our young people face. Of course there is intrinsic joy in creative and cultural education. In that sense it needs no justification. But let's also explore the extrinsic purpose of creative education – self-fulfilment and heightened expectation.

---

10 Garmezy, N., 'Resiliency and vulnerability to adverse developmental outcomes associated with poverty', *American Behavioral Scientist*, 34(4) (1991); Mehan, H., Hubbard, L., Villanueva, I., 'Forming academic identities: Accommodation without assimilation among involuntary minorities', *Anthropology and Education Quarterly*, 25(2) (1994); Fry, P. S., 'Pupil performance under varying teacher conditions of high and low expectations and high and low controls', *Canadian Journal of Behavioural Science*, Vol. 14(3) (1982).

Creative and cultural education is one of the most effective catalysts for the vital life-chemistry of ambition, confidence and expectation.

Consider the evidence from OFSTED in their inspection of creative learning. The OFSTED report on how Creative Partnerships – at the heart of which is creative learning inspired by creative practitioners working in schools – has routinely unlocked expectations of pupils, teachers, parents and carers. Quantifiable improvements in attendance, attainment levels and parental involvement result from this.

> 'The most effective programmes had a real purpose that motivated teachers and pupils, regardless of their prior experience. For many pupils, the high quality of the experience was directly related to the unpredictable approaches taken by creative practitioners working with teachers and the different relationships that developed. Pupils were particularly inspired by opportunities to work directly in the creative industries. Such involvement gave them high aspirations for the future.'[11]

It is not only the expectations of teachers and pupils that are recalibrated through creative and cultural education but those of parents too. It is clearly established that parental involvement in their child's learning is a vital factor in the child's success.[12] This was prompted by observations that children communicate their enjoyment of school-based creative projects to their parents to a much greater extent than

---

11 'Learning: creative approaches that raise standards', OFSTED (January 2010).
12 Safford, K. and O'Sullivan, O., 'Their Learning becomes your journey: Parents respond to children's work in Creative Partnerships', Centre for Literacy in Primary Education (2007).

their work in the core curriculum. The creative curriculum has a positive impact on home-school communications as parents develop perspectives on their children as learners and also on their own learning, past and present. Creative programmes offer low-risk invitations that encourage parents to engage with teachers and the whole school. While some parents may lack confidence to support their children in literacy and numeracy (particularly perhaps as mathematics is so different from their own school learning), they feel able to extend creative programmes at home.

It is not only the expectations of teachers and pupils that are recalibrated through creative and cultural education but those of parents too.

Let us take you back to the National Portrait Gallery in 2005 to an exhibition called 'Family Faces'. This exhibition came about after more than sixty families in seven Haringey schools worked with a ceramicist. These were whole family groups, with children taking part alongside parents, carers, grandparents and siblings. Each family produced a sculpture of itself. These sculptures, accompanied by the participants' commentaries on the experience, formed a display at the gallery as part of its 'Reaching Out, Drawing In' initiative, which was supported by the Heritage Lottery Fund. Those of us fortunate enough to visit that exhibition saw the outputs of a truly creative and memorable experience for those children and families. It was a scheme driven by principles of personal confidence, family learning, cultural identity and respect, problem solving, critical reflection – and celebration.

The sculptures were colourful, well crafted, funny and sad. All were compelling accounts of human drama in those Haringey families. But the written commentaries were even more significant. When one child was asked where his ideas had come from, he responded, 'From my dreams.'

The expectations to which we refer in this chapter are broadly based – they are of the self as well as of others. They relate to the development of well-being, resilience and self-identity in young people. This is well expressed by Alex Farquharson, Director of Nottingham Contemporary, which has developed an ambitious learning programme for young people:

'This is a place of lifelong learning, encompassing all audiences from toddlers to the retired. This is where we expect wonderful new vistas to be opened up to students of all ages – a space where the world will be imagined differently, in keeping with the mission of Nottingham Contemporary.' [13]

This ambition is supported by Daniel Fujiwara in his report on the value of participating in museums and the arts. Alongside his exact figures on the financial value of cultural engagement, his study is a confirmation of the reality and importance of that value.[14]

At the root of the nation's creativity is our propensity to tell and love stories. Storytelling is one of the first creative activities shared by parents and children, and then developed within the school and further education system. No nation has such a panoply of great fictional storytellers for children of all ages, backgrounds and nationalities. These stories, often creating new worlds, are exported to all parts of the globe.

At the Story Museum in Oxford recently, an exhibition called '26 Characters' brought together twenty-six (the number of letters in the alphabet) famous writers for children.

13 Farquharson, Alex, from the prospectus for the opening of Nottingham Contemporary, 2009.
14 Fujiwara, Daniel, 'Museums and happiness: The value of participating in museums and the arts', Museum of East Anglian Life/Arts Council England (2013).

These authors were then photographed in costume as their favourite characters from childhood reading – Peter Pan, the Mad Hatter, Long John Silver and so on. World-renowned authors such as Philip Pullman, Michael Morpurgo and Julia Donaldson pass on their own passions for reading and writing in this and other ways. Authors such as J. K. Rowling and J. R. R. Tolkien are among the best-known cultural figures in the world. And it should be noted that these are individuals who generate multi-million-pound industries around them through film, television and games as well as their books. They become inspirations for young people who will become future players in the global creative landscape.

We know that many young people make profound self-limiting decisions at around the age of twelve or thirteen. We owe it to them to broaden their horizons, develop their self-esteem and build their resilience particularly in their teenage years. A creative cultural education has a special contribution to make in this respect.

Chapter 6

FROM 'STEM' TO 'STEAM' AND BEYOND

Expectations should be set high, recognising that cultural education subjects are not easy options. The skills developed have a positive impact on overall academic achievement, as demonstrated in many studies. The USA, in particular, has argued the case for the value of cultural education in the lives of young people. In the UK much has been written about the importance of STEM subjects (Science, Technology, Engineering and Mathematics). We support those advocating STEAM, with Arts included in the grouping. But we need to focus beyond the education sector to make a true assessment of cultural education's value. The creative industries, relying on the output of the system, need a growing supply of creative people to maintain their global pre-eminence. These people will come through the education system – and the creative industries also benefit from the magnetic effect of the UK's global reputation in this area.

Cultural education subjects in schools should not be seen as an easy option and therefore for less academically able children. They add to the sum of academic achievement and knowledge of a pupil, as well as helping them to learn skills, which will benefit them both as individuals in their adult life and as potential employees in the world of work. Academically able young people should not be steered away from subjects that might form the basis for their future employment within the creative and cultural industries, rather they should be studied alongside subjects such as English, mathematics, the sciences and foreign languages.

The UK has an excellent reputation on the international stage for its creative output. It can be argued that our influence on literature, design, cinema, theatre, museums, the visual arts, music and the presentation of our heritage assets internationally is disproportionately large for a country of our relatively small size. These are also areas in which we have traditionally been admired from abroad for our achievements in the related education sector. It would be highly regrettable if this international reputation for excellence were allowed to decline in any way.

Any downgrading of investment in the area of cultural education or in the status of the subjects that are required by the creative and cultural industries for future employees could pose a serious risk to the revenues earned by UK plc.

It is significant that China, Singapore and other emerging economies place great store in strengthening their own cultural education as one of the building blocks for investing in the future of their countries. These nations are shifting their economies and education objectives to a position where they will no longer be known for the 'Made in . . . ' label but for 'Created in China', 'Designed in Singapore'.

We should take this shift seriously, recognising that the UK has both the experience and potential to compete internationally in this area. The CBI has argued:

> 'The creative sector has huge growth potential . . . The digital and creative industries are a natural export strength for the UK, providing the UK's third largest export sector – only behind advanced engineering and financial and professional services.'[14]

As the driving force behind the commissioning of the Henley Reviews into Music Education and Cultural Education in 2011 and 2012, the Minister for Culture and Digital Industries, Ed Vaizey MP, has been a consistent supporter of the need for investment in cultural education, saying:

---

14 'Skills for the Creative Industries: Investing in the Talents of our People', CBI (2011).

'Learning about culture and having opportunities to take part offers huge rewards to young people. Our culture brings audiences from across the world and we are particularly adept at producing world-leading performers and artists. To remain in such a strong position we need to be sure that we are giving children the best start in their cultural education. This should not just be an optional extra, but an essential part of every child's school life.'

Independent careers advice given to young people who wish to work in the creative and cultural industries by their schools should be of a high standard, with particular reference to fast-developing areas of technology. It is imperative that young people are made aware of the full range of opportunities available to them across the creative and cultural industries – particularly those careers that operate 'behind the scenes' away from the glare of publicity, which might not immediately be apparent to a young person considering their options for the world of work. Independent careers guidance provided through their schools should help young people to gain knowledge of available jobs, as well as informing them of the subjects that they need to study to stand the best chance of gaining skilled employment in their chosen area. It is also important that careers advice signposts young people towards the right further and higher education courses to enable them to increase the probability of gaining employment.

The skills that children acquire through good cultural education help to develop their personality, abilities and imagination. They allow them to learn how to think both creatively and critically and to express themselves fully. All these skills are strong influencers on wider academic attainment in schools and help to grow a child's interest in the process of learning within the school environment.

A report published by the Culture and Sport Evidence Programme underlined the positive effect that cultural education could have on young people's overall academic attainment:

> 'Participation in structured arts activities improves young people's cognitive abilities . . . Participation of young people in such activities could increase their cognitive ability test scores by 16 per cent and 19 per cent, on average, above that of non-participants (all other things being equal).'[15]

The expert panel for England's National Curriculum Review, chaired by Tim Oates, recognised that art and music lessons not only have 'intrinsic worth' in their own

---

15 'Understanding the impact of engagement in culture and sport', Culture and Sport Evidence Programme (2010). (This joint programme of strategic research was led by the Department for Culture, Media and Sport in collaboration with Arts Council England, English Heritage and Sport England.)

right, but also bring 'benefits to pupil engagement, cognitive development and achievement, including in mathematics and reading'.[16]

A report from the USA, published by the President's Committee on the Arts and Humanities (the First Lady, Michelle Obama, is the Honorary Chairman) contains a good deal of research from American schools, which provides a series of clear and compelling arguments as to the value of cultural education in the lives of young people:

'The study of drama, dance, music and the visual arts helps students explore realities, relationships, and ideas that cannot be conveyed simply in words or numbers. The ability to perform and create in the fine arts engenders innovative problem-solving skills that students can apply to other academic disciplines and provides experiences working as a team. Equally important, arts instruction supports success in other subjects.'[17]

The American report discusses seven studies identified by the Arts Education Partnership showing 'the pattern between high levels of arts participation and higher grades

---

16 'The Framework for the National Curriculum Review', Department for Education (2011).
17 'Reinvesting in Arts Education: Winning America's Future Through Creative Schools', President's Committee on the Arts and Humanities (2011).

and test scores in math and reading.'[18] An analysis of data from the National Educational Longitudinal Survey (NELS), which looked at the results of 25,000 students over a ten-year span, was profound:

> 'Students with high involvement in the arts, including minority and low-income students, performed better in school and stayed in school longer than students with low involvement, the relative involvement increasing over the school years. Low-income students involved in band and orchestra out-scored others on the NELS math assessment; low-income students involved in drama showed greater reading proficiency and more positive self-concept compared to those with little or no involvement.'[19]

Follow-up research published by the Arts Education Partnership reported on sixty-two separate research studies:

> '. . . many of which found transfer of skills from the arts (visual arts, dance, drama, music, multi-arts) to learning in other subject areas'.[20]

---

18 Fiske, E., 'Champions of Change: The impact of the arts on learning', Arts Education Partnership, Washington DC (1999).
19 'Reinvesting in Arts Education: Winning America's Future Through Creative Schools', President's Committee on the Arts and Humanities (2011).
20 Deasy, Richard J., 'Critical Links: Learning in the Arts and Student Academic and Social Development', Arts Education Partnership, Washington DC (2002).

The report by the President's Committee on the Arts and Humanities also identifies recent research in the area of arts and neuro-science, 'in particular . . . the complex ways that certain types of arts experience effect cognitive development'.[21] Findings include:

'Music training is closely correlated with development of phonological awareness – one of the most important predictors of early reading skills. Children who were motivated to practice a specific art form developed improved attention and also improved general intelligence. Training of attention and focus leads to improvement in other cognitive domains.'[22]

Much has been written about the importance of the 'STEM' subjects (Science, Technology, Engineering and Mathematics), although we would add our names to the growing list of advocates for 'STEM' to become 'STEAM', with 'Arts' being included in this grouping.

The 2011 'Next Gen' review by Ian Livingstone and Alex Hope for NESTA into the video games and visual effects industries identified 'severe misalignments between the education system and what the UK video games and

---

21 'Reinvesting in Arts Education: Winning America's Future Through Creative Schools', President's Committee on the Arts and Humanities (2011).
22 Ibid.

visual effects industries need'.[23] They go on to argue that there should be greater crossover between art and science within education, with the current structure based on the nineteenth-century faculty system. They also note that this separation is not in existence in fast-developing economies, such as Singapore.

The findings of the Livingstone-Hope Review were echoed by Eric Schmidt, the Executive Chair of Google, when he gave the MacTaggart Lecture in 2011:

'Over the past century, the UK has stopped nurturing its polymaths. You need to bring art and science back together . . . Lewis Carroll didn't just write one of the classic fairy tales of all time. He was also a mathematics tutor at Oxford. James Clerk Maxwell was described by Einstein as among the best physicists since Newton – but he was also a published poet.'

As one recent example of good practice, from the Saturday Club programme, young people explored a range of subject areas at the world's leading museum of art and design, the V&A in London. The areas explored included ceramic press moulding, textile design using sewing machines,

23 Livingstone, Ian and Hope, Alex, 'Next Gen: Transforming the UK into the world's leading talent hub for the video games and visual effects industries', NESTA (2011).

Cultural education influences and gives practical reality to other subject areas in the core curriculum.

print design, upholstery and furniture making. As part of the course, former V&A Sound Art Resident Jason Singh delivered a sound project that involved navigating around the museum using different sounds. There was also a Masterclass with designer Moritz Waldemeyer, who worked with the young people to make LED circuit boards that they turned into lights. It was challenging, inspiring and exciting; and it also demonstrated how cultural education influences and gives practical reality to other subject areas in the core curriculum. Such projects develop skills and open up opportunities to think differently: these lay the groundwork for future careers in the creative industries.

The challenge for the cultural education offer in schools is not just the formal one through the subjects on the curriculum. There are also countless informal offers. The issue is usually getting them to scale up, moving beyond local prototypes to national programmes. The will is there in the creative industries that have a vested interest in educating future participants, but more needs to be done to formalise this. It will be a helpful step forward to bring arts and science closer together through cultural education – to move from STEM to STEAM and beyond, to integrate the need for creativity into the curriculum alongside literacy and numeracy.

Beyond the school system, we need to enable better links with higher and further education, and then with the creative industries – the Kebab Stick approach we described in Chapter 2. Better careers advice is part of the solution, and this needs a nationwide programme to help teachers be in the loop with better information. However, it needs proper planning because, for example, in design alone there is an array of disciplines (more than twenty) that can be baffling to those not steeped in them and not able to follow the constant shifting of specialist knowledge.

The great tertiary educational establishments, particularly of art and design, bring new graduates into the creative industries each year, with two and a half million people now working in that sector. You cannot have creativity, you cannot have world-leading creative industries, without creative people. This extends beyond a commitment to our home-grown talent to the necessity of acknowledging and indeed encouraging a multinational creative community in the UK. We are fortunate in our geographical position; we are also open to trade and inward investment, making the country an international hub for creativity and commerce.

The World Bank ranks the UK as the easiest place in Europe to set up and run a business. So our creative strengths, and commitment to supporting future growth, continue to convince international companies to locate in the UK – for example, for design, like Nissan and Panasonic, or for film and television, like Viacom. Our multinational design community, with talented creative people drawn from all around the world but with a British core, is a competitive strength because it is a magnet for creative people on a global basis. In effect we have a kind of greenhouse, full of imaginative, skilled people who bring different cultures and perspectives, whose ideas cross-fertilise in a unique, dynamic infrastructure.

This is the shape of the future creative industries, this is the world we are moving into. We need to embrace it.

Chapter 7

WHAT CULTURAL EDUCATION SHOULD A CHILD EXPERIENCE?

*Children and young people should expect
to experience a wide range of cultural
education. We set out the minimum levels
they should receive at the ages of seven,
eleven and sixteen years old, together with
the expectations when a young person leaves
school at the age of eighteen. The adoption of
these levels would result in culturally literate
and creative generations ready to move into
adulthood. Head teachers have a vital role to
play in working with cultural organisations
and developing two-way relationships. Such
work with organisations and individuals will
augment, not replace, cultural education in
schools. Artists-in-residence should not just
be visual artists but drawn from a wider
spectrum. Our belief, and all the evidence
from the best schools, suggests that high
standards of cultural education (and its
influence across the curriculum) create better
possibilities for learning and behaviour
within schools.*

In this chapter we outline the spectrum of cultural education and the expectations for what children and young people will receive during their schooling as a whole. For children to leave full-time education without having engaged in the spectrum of cultural education outlined here would be a failure of a system which sets out to create young people who are not only academically able, but also have a fully-rounded appreciation of the world around them.

In her 2011 independent report for the government on Early Years provision, Dame Clare Tickell clearly lays out a rationale for delivering cultural education to the very youngest children:

'Alongside the three prime areas of personal, social and emotional development, communication and language, and physical development, I propose four specific areas in which prime skills are applied: literacy, mathematics, expressive arts and design, and understanding the world. Practitioners working with the youngest children should focus on the prime areas, but also recognise that the foundations of all areas of learning are laid from birth – for example literacy in the very early sharing of books, and mathematics through early experiences of quantity and spatial relationships. Any focus on the prime areas will be complemented and reinforced by learning in the specific areas, for example expressive arts is a key route through which children develop language and physical skills.'[24]

By the time a child is **seven** years old, they should have:

• Regularly taken part in different cultural activities, such as reading books and storytelling, arts and crafts, making short animations, singing, music-making, acting and dance.

• They should also have been given the opportunity to visit age-appropriate events and venues, such as a theatre, cinema, concert hall, museum, gallery, library or heritage site.

By the time a child is **eleven** years old, they should have enjoyed a high-quality curriculum offer that includes:

• The opportunity to gain knowledge about cultural education subjects and also to explore their own creativity.

• The chance to create, to design, to devise, to compose and to choreograph their own work in collaboration with their classmates.

---

24 Tickell, Clare, 'The Early Years: Foundations for life, health and learning', Department for Education (2011).

- The experience of creating work by themselves, such as writing a story, poem or play text.

- Presenting, displaying and performing to a range of audiences.

- Using arts-specific vocabulary to respond to, evaluate, explain, analyse, question and critique their own and other people's artistic works.

- Learning about the application of the latest technology to help them to access culture.

In addition, they will have:

- Been encouraged to be adventurous in their choices about cultural activities, by learning about literature, films, visual arts, crafts, heritage, drama, music and dance that is beyond the scope of their normal everyday engagement.

- Learned about the people who have created or are creating art forms. They will also have gained knowledge about the historical development of those art forms.

- Had the chance to learn a musical instrument.

- Regularly taken part in singing.

- Taken part in dramatic performances.

- Taken part in workshops with professional artists, craftsmen, architects, musicians, archivists, curators, dancers, film-makers, poets, authors or actors.

- Been on visits at each Key Stage to cultural institutions and venues, which might include a museum, a theatre, a gallery, a heritage site and a cinema.

- Become a regular user of a library.

- Regularly read books for pleasure, rather than only as part of their schoolwork.

- Been encouraged to use digital technology as a means of accessing and gaining a deeper understanding of great culture.

- Taken part in the making (writing, acting, shooting, editing) of a short film.

- Had the opportunity to gain an Arts Award qualification at the 'Discover' and 'Explore' levels.

- Received the support necessary to take an interest or passion further.

- Been made aware of the other activities and resources available to them in their local area.

- Been able to join a lunchtime or after-school club to continue their interests.

By the time a child is **sixteen** years old, they should have continued to have enjoyed a high-quality and enriching curriculum offer through Key Stage 3, including art, dance, drama, design, history, literature and music.

They should also have:

- Been given the opportunity to study cultural education subjects to gain qualifications at Level 2.

- Continued their journey of cultural discovery by being encouraged to make adventurous choices about the cultural activities they enjoy.

- Developed a knowledge about the range of different aspects of culture, including an understanding of the historical development and context of art, drama, design, literature and music.

- Developed an understanding of the different forms of each cultural area (for example: literature includes poetry, play texts, short stories and novels; music genres include classical, pop, hip hop, rock, jazz, folk, musical theatre and world).

- Been on regular visits to a museum, heritage site, gallery and cinema at each Key Stage.

- Sung in the school choir.

- Attended professional concerts and plays.

- Taken part in an artistic performance.

- Watched and learned about films from outside of the mainstream 'Hollywood blockbusters', with a specific emphasis on British film.

- Read a broad range of books both by living authors and by authors who may no longer be alive, but whose books are regarded as literary classics. Some of these books might be about subjects that are directly relevant to the readers' lives today, but young people should also be reading books that expand their horizons and show them the possibilities in the world beyond their own direct experiences.

- Continued to use a library to access a wide range of books, as well as for other research materials.

- Regularly made use of digital technology to see, read and listen to great culture, no matter where it is situated in the world.

- Had their artistic and creative work celebrated in school and in their wider local community through publication, exhibitions, performance and screenings.

- Had the opportunity to achieve their Arts Award Gold, supporting progression to further and higher education and employment.

- Been supported to take particular talents and interests forward.

- Had a chance to learn about careers in the creative and cultural industries and been supported to find work experience in these areas, should they wish to pursue it.

- Had the chance to lead or shape activity in school by helping with a club, acting as an 'arts mentor' or helping in the school library.

- Been able to join a lunchtime or after-school club in areas such as creative writing, dance, drama, art, music, film or digital media.

By the time a young person leaves school at the age of **eighteen** or **nineteen** years old, they should additionally have:

- Been given the opportunity to study cultural education subjects to gain qualifications at Level 3.

- Been made aware of apprenticeships offered by Creative & Cultural Skills (the Sector Skills Council for craft, cultural heritage, design, literature, music, performing and visual arts) and Skillset (the Sector Skills Council for TV, film, radio, interactive media, animation, computer games, facilities, photo imaging, publishing, advertising, fashion and textiles).

- Had the opportunity to spend time interacting with cultural professionals (such as artists, writers, archivists, musicians, curators, technicians, film-makers, actors, designers and dancers).

- Learned about the wider world of employment opportunities within the creative and cultural industries, beyond the examples of well-known personalities who are front-line performers or 'big name' creative practitioners.

- Been encouraged to continue to sample a wide range of adventurous cultural experiences during their own leisure time.

- Been encouraged to take part in the broad range of cultural events that take place both within their school environment and in the wider area in which they live.

- Developed the ability to build on the knowledge, which they have acquired about culture, to be able to discuss and critique the new cultural works that they encounter.

- Had their own personal achievements in cultural activities celebrated in school or in their wider local community.

The adoption of these minimum levels of expectation across the education system would result in a generation of culturally aware and culturally literate young people moving into adulthood with a genuine understanding of culture and the ability to make informed critical decisions about the cultural activities in which they engage later in their lives. Parents and carers should be encouraged to engage with their children's schools in making demands in relation to minimum expectations of delivery in this area.

The Arts Award developed by Arts Council England and accredited by Trinity College London, with the support of the Arts Council's network of ten regional bridge organisations, helps young people to develop as artists and arts leaders in areas such as the performing arts, visual arts, literature, media and multimedia. This award is made at Bronze, Silver and Gold levels, and is aimed at young people aged eleven and above. Additionally, there is an Arts Award 'Discover' level for children aged between five and seven, alongside an Arts Award 'Explore' level for those aged between seven and eleven. These are both valuable and valued qualifications and all schools should consider offering them as part of a general programme of cultural enrichment.

Head teachers have an increasingly important role to play in the commissioning of cultural organisations to work in partnership with their schools. Cultural organisations need to continue to build closer relationships directly with head teachers, so that a dialogue can be opened and maintained. More and more, cultural organisations regard engagement with potential sponsors from the business community in their local area as part of their everyday job. However, they do not always recognise the importance of head teachers in terms of building relationships that could deliver incremental revenue streams for their organisations.

The dialogue between schools and the cultural organisations working with schools must be meaningful – and two-way.

The dialogue between schools and the cultural organisations working with schools must be meaningful – and two-way. The cultural organisations need to ensure that the programmes and activities they provide are fulfilling the requirements identified by the schools; the schools themselves need to articulate their requirements clearly to the cultural organisations. Quality, standards and learning outcomes should be the watchwords for all cultural organisations' engagement with schools.

Arts educators should exist to augment and broaden the work of classroom teachers.

We must stress here that cultural organisations should not be expected to replace formal cultural education in schools. Arts educators should exist to augment and broaden the work of classroom teachers, rather than be a replacement. A visit to a museum or gallery should not be viewed as a replacement for classroom-based learning (nor merely as an outing at the end of term). In the same way, visits from musicians or writers should form only part of a young person's learning, alongside the valuable work of their classroom teacher.

There is a good deal of benefit to be gained for schools, pupils and teachers in building long-term, high-quality relationships with specific artists from across all art forms. This could be via artist-in-residence schemes, whereby an artist spends a meaningful amount of time working in a school across all year groups. This increases the likelihood of young people gaining a greater understanding of the work and effort necessary over a sustained period to create great art. For the avoidance of doubt, the suggestion here is not that only visual artists would be able to fulfil this role; it would be as appropriate for poets, dancers, film-makers and the like.

One measure of a school's commitment to cultural education is the Artsmark Award, developed by Arts Council England and delivered by Trinity College London, with the ten regional bridge organisations driving participation. It covers art and design, dance, drama, music and creative writing, with 15 per cent of schools in England holding the award. It focuses on the quantity, quality and impact of education work by cultural organisations. This is not to be confused with the Arts Award, which is also operated by Arts Council England and Trinity College London. This centres on the individual child, whereas the Artsmark is awarded to schools.

Despite wishing to see cultural education subjects recognised for their own intrinsic worth, it would be remiss of us not to note that our best-achieving schools tend to offer a high standard of cultural education to their pupils, with excellent facilities and teaching in areas such as art and design, design technology, music and the performing arts. This cultural activity – and the value placed upon it within the school environment – in itself creates a culture of learning and behaviour within schools. Alongside the primary benefit of learning about culture for its own sake, this has the secondary benefit of engaging many children with their general schooling to a far greater extent than might otherwise be the case.

However, simply increasing capacity in terms of making facilities and opportunities available to children and young people in schools should not be regarded as a 'quick fix'. It is also necessary to ensure that expectations of standards in school leadership and teaching of cultural education subjects are set at a high level in both curriculum subjects and in more informal in-school settings.

Chapter 8

THE FUTURE: NATIONAL COMMITMENT AND LOCAL LEADERSHIP

A national commitment to excellence in cultural education needs to be met by consistent, high-quality local delivery. New models, such as music education hubs and design Saturday clubs, show promise to bring new energy to cultural education. Some universities are providing visionary cultural leadership in cities like Hull and Liverpool. These forms of local leadership best overcome barriers to a vibrant cultural education for all young people, closing the gap for those who come from less advantaged backgrounds. The case for arts and cultural funding, as argued by all political parties, has to appeal to the widest possible public support: culture is not the preserve of the elite. Leadership is needed, through local authorities, universities, libraries, Arts Council England and all organisations involved, to open up opportunities for young people. Schools must be at the heart of this. An excellent cultural education is the right of everyone, bringing personal, social and commercial advantages that can only benefit the lives of all individuals in our society.

There remains a great deal of patchiness in the provision of cultural education across England. In some places, it is truly excellent with a well-honed partnership of schools, nationally funded organisations, enlightened local authority investment, charities and voluntary organisations coming together to give children great opportunities. In other areas, there is still a real dearth of provision.

In previous chapters we have argued the case for a strong and visible national commitment to cultural education. In this final chapter we explore how that needs to be matched by vibrant and distributed leadership of the local delivery of cultural education.

In many local areas, there remains a good deal of duplication of resources between different cultural organisations and venues. There are, however, encouraging examples of local leadership which develop economies of scale and joint operations between different organisations providing cultural education services. This means that the potential would increase for a greater amount of public money to be spent on delivering cultural education directly to children and young people, rather than on administrative costs.

The creation of a new network of Music Education Hubs across England is proving the benefit of a national commitment delivered through local leadership. Music education hubs are at an early stage of development but the most effective have added a new energy and coherence to music education. There is an increasing use of partners in the local music 'ecology' – partners offering new and more diverse opportunities, new sources of funding and clearer pathways for young people to progress their commitment to their own music-making. There are also examples of the music education hub practice being developed into wider cultural education hubs – for example at The Barbican Centre in the City of London.

The East London and City Culture Partnership brings together six hubs across eight boroughs and the City of London, Barbican Creative Learning, the Guildhall School of Music and Drama, and Arts Council England bridge organisation A New Direction as core partners. The partnership has three years of funding from the Esmée Fairbairn Foundation to develop itself and provide the framework for entitlement and progression in the area. Through Connected London, work is in progress with the Innovation Unit to test a number of partnership models. There are of course challenges in bringing different art forms together – in defining need, in overcoming the dominance of the supplier voice, and in establishing the means of ensuring consistent quality. These are issues which are focused on throughout the development process. In another area of cultural education, the Saturday clubs for young designers are forging new models at local levels through more highly developed relationships with universities and practitioners.

There are some visionary examples of higher-education institutions acting as the nucleus and catalyst for cultural education.

There are some visionary examples of higher-education institutions acting as the nucleus and catalyst for cultural education within their geographical area. The power of the potential that universities have as agents for cultural regeneration should be both recognised and celebrated. We have been particularly impressed by the work of the University of Hull in the important role it played in the city's successful bid to become UK City of Culture in 2017, and its sense of corporate responsibility for the cultural life of the city in which it is located.

Meanwhile, Liverpool John Moores University has an innovative scheme to involve its students in the cultural life of its home city, with partnerships with the Royal Liverpool Philharmonic Orchestra, the Everyman Theatre and Tate Liverpool, that will see many of its 25,000 students actively engaging with the city's cultural institutions for the first time.

The University of Nottingham and Nottingham Trent University have made a significant financial commitment to fund the public programme at Nottingham Contemporary – a programme of learning and research in contemporary art. Nottingham University Music Department has also been a key supporter of the Nottingham In Harmony programme through the provision of music undergraduates as mentors to the children involved in the programme.

In the more specialist music conservatoire sector, Birmingham Conservatoire, the Royal College of Music, Trinity Laban Conservatoire of Music and Dance, the Royal Northern College of Music, the Royal Academy of Music and Guildhall School of Music and Drama all play an active and meaningful role in their local music education hubs.

So why is the local leadership of cultural education so important? It is because at that level there is the best opportunity to overcome the existing barriers to our ambition of a vibrant cultural education for all children and young people. It is at that level that key challenges of equity, inclusion and quality can be met.

It is vital that our approach to cultural education 'closes the gap' between those children and young people who come from families who are more likely to access cultural provision and those children who come from backgrounds that mean they find it more challenging to make cultural activities and learning part of their everyday lives. There is startling evidence about the correlation between levels of parental educational achievement and their children's engagement with cultural activity at primary age. Some 70 per cent of children of parents with the lowest level of educational qualifications spent less than three hours per week on cultural activities, and 42 per cent spent no time at all. Meanwhile 80 per cent of children whose parents had degree-level qualifications spent more than three hours per week on cultural activity, and 27 per cent spent more than ten hours.[25] This challenge is best met at a local level where real understandings of local communities reside. The most effective local leadership would identify and respond to proven need, rather than simply concentrating on creating a structure for the supply of provision.

25 Evaluation of the Find Your Talent programme, Ipsos MORI, October 2009.

Embedded in this challenge are sensitive issues of inclusion, particularly for groups who are often under-represented in some cultural activities. This would include young people from certain minority ethnic backgrounds and young people with special educational needs. The best cultural programmes ensure the highest quality of experience for all – but this is by no means the norm. And rigorous inclusion in cultural activities depends on listening, and more importantly responding, to the voice of children and young people. Again, it is at the local level that those voices are most effective.

The moral argument for the value of culture in enriching the lives of individuals and communities – no matter what their economic background – is widely made and understood. However, there is a less often argued case, which is no less valuable; it draws on the world of business for its legitimacy. No business in its right mind would consider that it could have a healthy future if its client base and its workforce were to be as restricted as is the case with the arts sector. And yet, sections of the arts community appear to be quite happy to keep mass-market consumers out of the club. The risk of allowing this narrow focus of consumption and appreciation to continue is that the very art forms that the elite claims to be protecting will ultimately ossify, withering on the vine.

Rigorous inclusion in cultural activities depends on listening, and more importantly responding, to the voice of children and young people.

Concerns over accessibility to the arts cross political boundaries, with both the Conservative Secretary of State for Culture, Media and Sport, Rt Hon Sajid Javid MP, and the Labour Shadow, Rt Hon Harriet Harman MP, effectively arguing this case in separate policy speeches within a week of each other in June 2014.

Sajid Javid said:

'I want you to make what you do accessible to everyone. That doesn't mean striving for popularity and aiming for the lowest common denominator. It means ensuring that everyone in the UK has the opportunity to engage with our artists and actors, our history and heritage. It means giving everyone a chance to develop their own cultural tastes. Never forget that every penny of taxpayer support and lottery cash that goes to culture has been provided by hard-working people from every community in the UK.'[26]

A point echoed by Harriet Harman:

'Whilst in better times, it might have been possible to fund the arts without consciously engaging public support, that just isn't the case now. When the NHS is

---

26 https://www.gov.uk/government/speeches/culture-for-all

struggling, and councils face agonising choices about cutting care for dementia sufferers – public funding for the arts is only sustainable to the extent that the public know it matters for them. And the public will not support the arts, especially at such difficult times for family and public finances, if there's even a suspicion that it is disproportionately something for the elite, for a privileged few. We all have to turn and address this big issue. If you are getting public money, people have to have a stake in what you do. So we have to have a genuine and visible widening of access and inclusion.'[27]

As the figures above show, it is the 'demand' issue that is more pressing than 'supply'. The real challenge is how to increase demand from children and families who do not currently engage with creative and cultural opportunities. Too much of the debate is dominated by the vested interests of the supplier voice. The real prize is to close the gap between those who have a rich creative and cultural experience and those for whom it simply does not exist. It can be done. It involves well-evidenced targeted use of funds, a real determination to put the voice of children and young people at the heart of planning and provision, and a strong and sustained engagement with families. This

---

27 http://press.labour.org.uk/post/88265413304/speech-on-young-people-and-the-arts-by-harriet-harman

is most effectively implemented at local level – especially at a time of such high levels of devolution to schools. It is too important to be an accident associated with individual schools and geography.

This approach requires strong and consistent leadership from all the partners committed to a broad-based and accessible cultural experience for young people. Creative intention and creative pedagogy count for little in the absence of creative leadership.

There are many partners in such local leadership. For example, the role of local authority-funded library services in the delivery of cultural education hubs should not be underestimated. Library services are already embedded into their local communities and often link communities, schools and cultural organisations. People who do not otherwise connect with cultural organisations trust them, and they tend not to be seen as being elitist. As well as having a direct input into the literature strand of cultural education, libraries are also excellent repositories of information about services available to young people in any given area and also have the technology available to enable young people to register on a database (through their library cards), which could be used to support other digitally led progammes.

Similarly critical is the contribution to cultural education by the National Portfolio Organisations (NPOs) and twenty-one Major Partner Museums funded by Arts Council England. Each NPO, in its funding agreement with the Arts Council, has made a commitment as to how it will ensure that 'Every child and young person has the opportunity to experience the richness of the arts, museums and libraries'.[28] There is scope for Arts Council England to be more demanding that NPOs deliver on these commitments and do so in a way that enhances the coherence and quality of the cultural offer at a local level.

And at the heart of all this must be schools, their head teachers and governing bodies or trustees. No school that ignores its responsibility to provide a powerful cultural education for its pupils can claim to be meeting its pupils' needs. No group of governors or trustees can claim to be meeting the needs of its local community if it fails to call its head teacher to account for the quality and range of the school's cultural education.

We are held up as a beacon of excellence in many other nations around the globe. Now is the time to continue to build on the firm foundations that are already laid in the area of cultural education. We need to ensure that every

---

28 Goal Five of Arts Council England's Strategic Framework 'Great Art and Culture for Everyone'.

child passing through our education system is able to benefit from the life-changing experiences and unique learning opportunities offered in areas as diverse as archaeology, architecture and the built environment, archives, craft, dance, design, digital arts, drama and theatre, film and cinemas, galleries, heritage, libraries, literature, live performance, museums, music, poetry and the visual arts.

There is so much that we already do that is right in creative and cultural education in this country. It is imperative that we build on this for future generations so that we remain a world-leading creative nation.

Chapter 9

SUMMARY OF THE ARGUMENT

1 There is a wide range of cultural education offered to children and young people across the UK. It operates through the formal education system, but also relies on other partnerships with organisations and people who add enormous value to the education. Cultural education is vital to the reinforcement of the UK's position as a world-leading creative nation, with all its social and commercial benefits. But there is a need for clearer pathways for children to gain the maximum benefit from cultural education. There remains a danger that talented individuals fail to achieve their potential for reasons of ethnicity, financial deprivation and geography.

2 Creativity is at the heart of the nation's identity and crucial to future economic development. We need to nurture and invest in creativity to compete in the global marketplace. The UK has a historical advantage, as a creative nation with world-leading creative industries, that we need to build upon for the future. Cultural education throughout the education system is crucial in developing creativity. Indeed, as well as literacy and numeracy, creativity needs to be seen as a fundamental educational objective that applies to every subject and helps every aspect of learning.

3 Every child should receive the best cultural education. This education should provide knowledge about culture's past, develop understanding and critical faculties, and enhance skills through practice in significant art forms. Other emotional and relationship benefits result from these, teaching lessons that apply to other areas of life. But high-quality interactions are essential, with schools best placed to ensure quality and champion diversity. Cultural education should encourage individual and collaborative abilities, grounded in the knowledge of the past (with visits to cultural places vital) but committed to the exploration of the present and the future (with digital technology playing an enabling role). Although all cultural education should be of the highest academic and vocational standards, it should also be fun.

4 Our ambition is for a challenging and inspiring creative education. Young people need to be considered more fully as the consumers of such an education. The benefits that accrue to them as individuals have a beneficial impact on society as a whole, because cultural education will create generations that are more inquisitive, persistent, imaginative, disciplined and collaborative – essential qualities for the future. The result will be generations of job-creators, not just job-seekers, vital for a world of continuous and rapid change. Creative learning therefore needs to be seen as a core teaching aim in all subjects.

5 Setting expectations high is important in enabling children to achieve their potential through education. Evidence shows that teacher and parental expectation is a cornerstone of pupil success. Creative and cultural education are important in raising such expectations, acting as catalysts for life-changing experiences that have a positive impact on the ambition and confidence of young people. Parents also find it easier and more productive to support their children in creative programmes at home, making education a more natural aspect of a rounded life. Cultural institutions have vital roles to play in adding breadth and depth to the school experience, broadening horizons for pupils particularly at times when low self-esteem, for example in the early teenage years, can lead to decisions that limit educational achievement.

6 Expectations should be set high, recognising that cultural education subjects are not easy options. The skills developed have a positive impact on overall academic achievement, as demonstrated in many studies. The USA, in particular, has argued the case for the value of cultural education in the lives of young people. In the UK, much has been written about the importance of STEM subjects (Science, Technology, Engineering and Mathematics). We support those advocating STEAM, with Arts included in the grouping. But we need to focus beyond the education sector to make a true assessment of cultural education's value. The creative industries, relying on the output of the system, need a growing supply of creative people to maintain their global pre-eminence. These people will come through the education system – and the creative industries also benefit from the magnetic effect of the UK's global reputation in this area.

7 Children and young people should expect to experience a wide range of cultural education. We set out the minimum levels they should receive at the ages of seven, eleven and sixteen years old, together with the expectations when a young person leaves school at the age of eighteen. The adoption of these levels would result in culturally literate and creative generations ready to move into adulthood. Head teachers have a vital role to play in working with cultural organisations and developing two-way relationships. Such work with organisations and individuals will augment, not replace, cultural education in schools. Artists-in-residence should not just be visual artists but drawn from a wider spectrum. Our belief, and all the evidence from the best schools, suggests that high standards of cultural education (and its influence across the curriculum) create better possibilities for learning and behaviour within schools.

8 A national commitment to excellence in cultural education needs to be met by consistent, high-quality local delivery. New models, such as music education hubs and design Saturday clubs, show promise to bring new energy to cultural education. Some universities are providing visionary cultural leadership in cities like Hull and Liverpool. These forms of local leadership best overcome barriers to a vibrant cultural education for all young people, closing the gap for those who come from less advantaged backgrounds. The case for arts and cultural funding, as argued by all political parties, has to appeal to the widest possible public support: culture is not the preserve of the elite. Leadership is needed, through local authorities, universities, libraries, Arts Council England and all organisations involved, to open up opportunities for young people. Schools must be at the heart of this. An excellent cultural education is the right of everyone, bringing personal, social and commercial advantages that can only benefit the lives of all individuals in our society.

About the authors

SIR JOHN SORRELL CBE is a UK business ambassador, appointed by successive prime ministers to promote Britain's Creative Industries abroad. He is co-chair of the Sorrell Foundation with Frances Sorrell (neé Newell). Since 1999 they have worked with tens of thousands of young people to inspire their creativity. John is chairman of University of the Arts London, Europe's specialist art and design university, with nearly 19,000 students from over 100 countries. He is also chairman of the London Design Festival, which he founded in 2003 and is founder and chairman of the Creative Industries Federation. Previously John was co-founder and chair of Newell and Sorrell, one of Europe's most successful design and identity businesses. He has had roles with a wide range of public and private sector organisations, including chairman of the UK Design Council, the Commission for Architecture and the Built Environment and the Design Business Association. John was awarded a knighthood in the 2008 New Year Honours List for services to the Creative Industries. He was appointed CBE in 1996 and was awarded the Royal Society of Arts Bicentenary Medal in 1998. He holds a number of Honorary Doctorates and Fellowships and his books, *Creative Island* (2002) and *Creative Island II* (2009), feature inspired design from Great Britain.

PAUL ROBERTS OBE graduated in philosophy and mathematics before becoming a teacher and a schools inspector. He was director of education in Nottingham and subsequently in Haringey, leading the government intervention in Haringey Council. He was a director of Capita Strategic Education Services before joining the Improvement and Development Agency (IDeA) for local government where he became managing director. As author of the report 'Nurturing Creativity in Young People', commissioned jointly by the Department for Education and Skills and the Department for Culture, Media and Sport, Paul was adviser to government ministers on the development of the cultural offer for young people and is now chair of the trustees for Creativity, Culture and Education. He is also chair of the Innovation Unit, vice-chair at Nottingham Contemporary and deputy chair at Mountview Academy of Theatre Arts. He is currently a member of the government's Cultural Education Board, of Arts Council England's steering group for In Harmony and a Commissioner for the University of Warwick Commission on the Future of Cultural Value. He is chair of the Nottingham Music Education Hub. Paul is a Fellow of the Royal Society of Arts and was appointed an OBE in 2008 for services to education and the Creative Industries.

DARREN HENLEY OBE is Managing Director of Classic FM, part of Global, the media and entertainment company also home to Heart, Capital, Capital XTRA, LBC, Smooth, Xfm and Gold. His two independent government reviews into music and cultural education resulted in the creation of England's first National Plan for Music Education, new networks of Music Education Hubs and Heritage Schools, the BFI Film Academy and the National Youth Dance Company. He chairs the government's Cultural Education Board and the Mayor of London's Music Education Advisory Group. A trustee of the exam board ABRSM, a Commissioner for the Warwick Commission on the Future of Cultural Value, and a vice president of the Canterbury Festival, he is the author of twenty-seven books. Darren is a Fellow of the Royal Society of Arts, the Radio Academy and the London College of Music; an Honorary Fellow of Canterbury Christ Church University and Trinity Laban Conservatoire of Music and Dance; an Honorary Member of the Royal Northern College of Music and the Incorporated Society of Musicians; and a Companion of the Chartered Management Institute. He holds honorary doctorates from the University of Hull, Birmingham City University and Buckinghamshire New University. The recipient of the Sir Charles Groves Prize for 'his outstanding contribution to British music', he was appointed an OBE in 2013 for services to music.

Acknowledgements

Although relatively short in length, in one way or another, this book has been a long time in the making. A huge number of people from the arts, education, business and political worlds have helped to shape our thinking over many years and we are enormously grateful to all of them for so willingly offering their insights to us. Special thanks to Lady Frances Sorrell for sharing many of her ideas and to Kirsty Leith, who was the guiding hand behind all three of the independent government reviews that this book draws upon. We also particularly want to thank John Simmons and David Carroll for helping to bring our words to life on the page – the first through his unrivalled editing skills and the second through his stunning design. For their patience and expertise, great thanks are also due to Lorne Forsyth, Olivia Bays, Jennie Condell, Pippa Crane and Thomas Ogilvie, who together make up the excellent team at our publisher, Elliott & Thompson.

Index

[158]